How Many Legs?

by Rebecca Weber

Here are some animals.

They use their legs to get around.

3

Here is a crab.

A crab has 10 legs.

It uses its legs to walk on sand.

This is a spider.
It has 8 legs.
It uses its legs
to move around.

Here is a ladybug.
It has 6 legs.

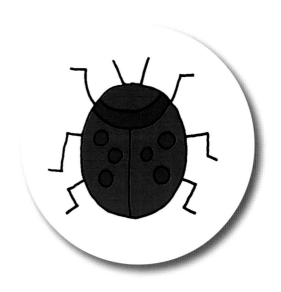

This ladybug uses its legs
to climb on a leaf.

Look at the lamb.

A lamb has 4 legs.

This lamb uses its legs
to walk in the grass.

This bat has 2 legs.
It uses its legs
to hang upside down.

13

Look! Here is a snake.

A snake does not have legs!

15

How do snakes get around?